THE FIFTY ~~STATES~~
FLA~~GS~~

P

State Names, Capital Cities, Areas and all other statistical information is based an data available as of February 2023. Population calculated using latest available estimate or latest available census data. We hope you enjoy using this book, if you have any queries, comments, corrections or other suggestions please send us an email to: enquires@flagsbook.com

INTRODUCTION

The United States of America is a federal republic made up of 50 states. A state in the United States is as a geographical boundary that holds legislative, executive, and judicial authority below the federal government.

This 2023 edition of Fifty States of the USA is a state by state guide with facts and updated demographics including Capitals & Largest Cities, Date Admitted to Union, Population and Area, State Anthems, Songs & Mottos, Demonyms (What inhabitants are known as), state trees, birds and flowers.

If you have enjoyed using this guide please consider leaving a review at Amazon or Goodreads. If you are interested in more flags facts and info then visit our website **flagsbook.com** and subscribe to our youtube channel **youtube.com/@flagsboo**k where we have videos about flags, U.S. and world geography and fun picture quizzes to test your knowledge.

THE AMERICAN FLAG

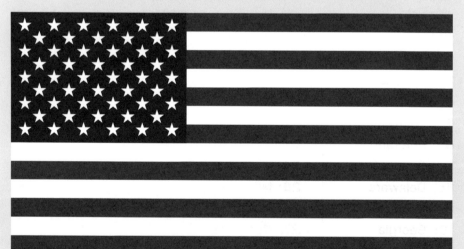

THE STARS AND STRIPES · RED, WHITE, AND BLUE
OLD GLORY · THE STAR-SPANGLED BANNER

Key to symbols used in this guide

 State Tree State Bird 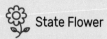 State Flower

STATES & ABBREVIATIONS

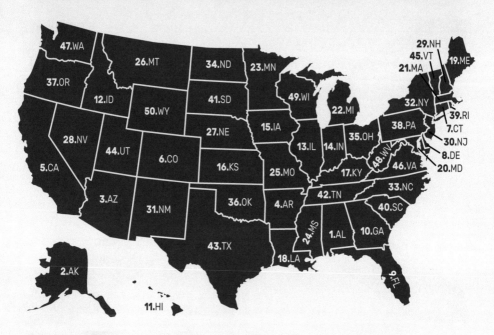

1:	Alabama	18:	Louisiana	35:	Ohio
2:	Alaska	19:	Maine	36:	Oklahoma
3:	Arizona	20:	Maryland	37:	Oregon
4:	Arkansas	21:	Massachusetts	38:	Pennsylvania
5:	California	22:	Michigan	39:	Rhode Island
6:	Colorado	23:	Minnesota	40:	South Carolina
7:	Connecticut	24:	Mississippi	41:	South Dakota
8:	Delaware	25:	Missouri	42:	Tennessee
9:	Florida	26:	Montana	43:	Texas
10:	Georgia	27:	Nebraska	44:	Utah
11:	Hawaii	28:	Nevada	45:	Vermont
12:	Idaho	29:	New Hampshire	46:	Virginia
13:	Illinois	30:	New Jersey	47:	Washington
14:	Indiana	31:	New Mexico	48:	West Virginia
15:	Iowa	32:	New York	49:	Wisconsin
16:	Kansas	33:	North Carolina	50:	Wyoming
17:	Kentucky	34:	North Dakota		

ALABAMA

THE YELLOWHAMMER STATE
THE HEART OF DIXIE · THE COTTON STATE

Capital: Montgomery

Largest City: Huntsville

Date Admitted to Union: December 14, 1819 *(22nd)*

Population: 5,024,279 *(24th Largest)*

Area: 52,419 sq mi (135,765 km^2) *(30th Largest)*

State Anthem /Song: "Alabama"

Motto: Audemus jura nostra defendere *(We dare defend our rights)*

Demonym: Alabamian, Alabaman

Quick Fact: Alabama became the first state to recognize Christmas a legal holiday, beginning the tradition in 1836.

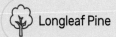 Longleaf Pine   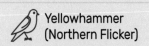 Yellowhammer (Northern Flicker)   Camellia

ALASKA

THE LAST FRONTIER

Capital: Juneau

Largest City: Anchorage

Date Admitted to Union: January 3, 1959 *(49th)*

Population: 736,081 *(48th Largest)*

Area: 663,268 sq mi (1,717,856 km²) *(1st Largest)*

State Anthem / Song: "Alaska's Flag"

Motto: North to the Future

Demonym: Alaskan

Quick Fact: *In Alaska, there is approx. 1 bear for every 21 people. Kodiak Island in Alaska is home to the Kodiak bear, it is the largest subspecies of the brown or grizzly bear and can grow to be 1,500 pounds and 10 feet tall standing on their hind legs.*

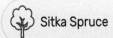 Sitka Spruce    Willow Ptarmigan    Forget Me Not

ARIZONA

THE GRAND CANYON STATE
THE COPPER STATE · THE VALENTINE STATE

Capital & Largest City: Phoenix

Date Admitted to Union: February 14, 1912 *(48th)*

Population: 7,151,502 *(14th Largest)*

Area: 113,990 sq mi (295,234 km²) *(6th Largest)*

State Anthem /Song: "The Arizona March Song", "Arizona"

Motto: Ditat Deus *(God enriches)*

Demonym: Arizonan

Quick Fact: Arizona is one of the four corner states along with New Mexico, Colorado, and Utah. You can be in all these states at the same time when you are at the four corners.

 Palo Verde   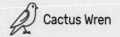 Cactus Wren   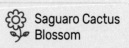 Saguaro Cactus Blossom

6

ARKANSAS

THE NATURAL STATE
LAND OF OPPORTUNITY

Capital & Largest City: Little Rock

Date Admitted to Union: June 15, 1836 *(25th)*

Population: 3,013,756 *(33rd Largest)*

Area: 53,179 sq mi (137,732 km^2) *(29th Largest)*

State Anthem /Song: "Arkansas", "The Arkansas Traveler" "Arkansas (You Run Deep in Me)", "Oh, Arkansas"

Motto: Regnat populus *(The People Rule)*

Demonym: Arkansan, Arkansawyer, Arkanite

Presidents: William Jefferson Clinton *(42nd)*

Quick Fact: Arkansas has the only active diamond mine in the US.

 Pine Tree   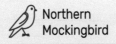 Northern Mockingbird   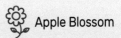 Apple Blossom

CALIFORNIA

GOLDEN STATE

Capital: Sacramento

Largest City: Los Angeles

Date Admitted to Union: September 9, 1850 *(31st)*

Population: 39,185,605 *(1st Largest)*

Area: 163,696 sq mi (423,970 km²) *(3rd Largest)*

State Anthem /Song: "I Love You, California"

Motto: Eureka

Demonym: Californian

Presidents: Richard Milhous Nixon *(37th)*

Quick Fact: California has 9 national parks, more than in any other state of the US.

 California Redwood & Sequoia   California Quail   Golden Poppy

COLORADO

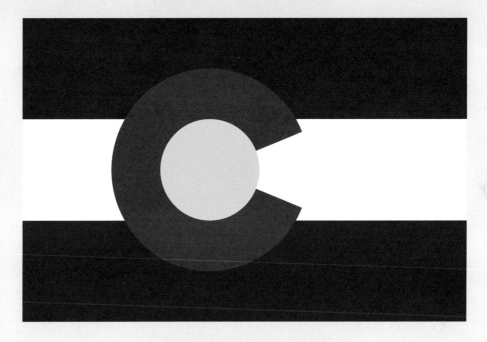

THE CENTENNIAL STATE

Capital & Largest City: Denver

Date Admitted to Union: August 1, 1876 *(38th)*

Population: 5,773,714 *(21st Largest)*

Area: 104,094 sq mi (269,837 km^2) *(8th Largest)*

State Anthem /Song: "Where the Columbines Grow",
"Rocky Mountain High"

Motto: Nil sine numine *(Nothing without providence)*

Demonym: Coloradan

Quick Fact: It is illegal to pick the state flower,
the Colorado Blue Columbine, on public lands
or without consent from a private land owner.

 Colorado
Blue Spruce

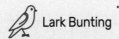 Lark Bunting

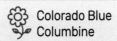 Colorado Blue
Columbine

CONNECTICUT

THE CONSTITUTION STATE · THE PROVISIONS STATE
THE NUTMEG STATE · THE LAND OF STEADY HABITS

Capital: Hartford

Largest City: Bridgeport

Date Admitted to Union: January 9, 1788 *(5th)*

Population: 3,605,944 *(29th Largest)*

Area: 5,018 sq mi (13,023 km²) *(48th Largest)*

State Anthem /Song: "Yankee Doodle"

Motto: Qui transtulit sustinet *(He who transplanted still sustains)*

Demonym: Connecticuter, Connecticutian, Nutmegger *(colloquial)*

Presidents: George Walker Bush *(43rd)*

Quick Fact: The name Connecticut means "long tidal river".

 White Oak   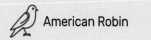 American Robin    Mountain Laurel

DELAWARE

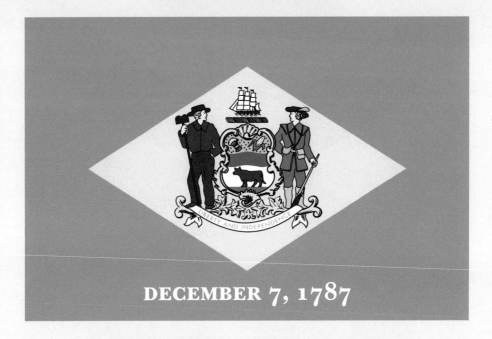

DECEMBER 7, 1787

THE FIRST STATE · THE SMALL WONDER
BLUE HEN STATE · THE DIAMOND STATE

Capital: Dover

Largest City: Wilmington

Date Admitted to Union: December 7, 1787 *(1st)*

Population: 1,003,384 *(45th Largest)*

Area: 2,489 sq mi (6,450 km²) *(49th Largest)*

State Anthem /Song: "Our Delaware"

Motto: Liberty and Independence

Demonym: Delawarean

Quick Fact: Is known as "The First State" as it was the first state to ratify the U.S. Constitution.

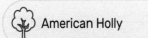 American Holly   Delaware Blue Hen   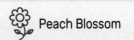 Peach Blossom

FLORIDA

SUNSHINE STATE

Capital: Tallahassee

Largest City: Jacksonville

Date Admitted to Union: March 3, 1845 *(27th)*

Population: 22,244,823 *(3rd Largest)*

Area: 65,758 sq mi (170,312 km^2) *(22nd Largest)*

State Anthem /Song: "Florida", "Old Folks at Home"

Motto: In God We Trust

Demonym: Floridian, Floridan

Quick Fact: Everglades National Park in Florida is the only place in the world that is home to both the American Crocodile and the American Alligator.

 Sabal Palm   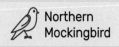 Northern Mockingbird   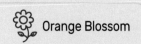 Orange Blossom

GEORGIA

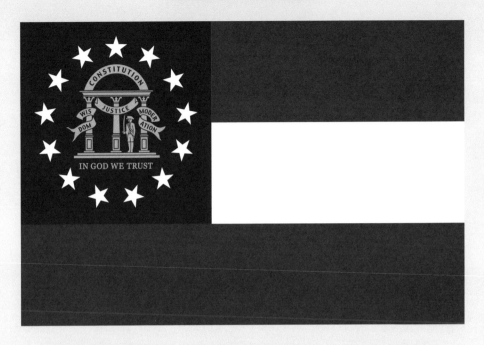

PEACH STATE • EMPIRE STATE OF THE SOUTH

Capital & Largest City: Atlanta

Date Admitted to Union: January 2, 1788 *(4th)*

Population: 10,711,908 *(8th Largest)*

Area: 59,425 sq mi (153,909 km²) *(24th Largest)*

State Anthem /Song: "Georgia on My Mind"

Motto: Wisdom, Justice, Moderation

Demonym: Georgian

Presidents: James Earl Jr. Carter *(39th)*

Quick Fact: Atlanta held the 1996 Summer Olympics. Also known as the Centennial Olympic Games, they marked the centenary of the 1896 Summer Olympics in Athens, Greece.

 Live Oak   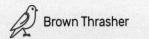 Brown Thrasher   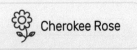 Cherokee Rose

HAWAII

THE ALOHA STATE · PARADISE OF THE PACIFIC
THE ISLANDS OF ALOHA · THE 808 STATE

Capital & Largest City: Honolulu

Date Admitted to Union: August 21, 1959 *(50th)*

Population: 1,455,271 *(40th Largest)*

Area: 10,931 sq mi (28,311 km²) *(47th Largest)*

State Anthem /Song: "Hawai'i Pono'ī" *(Hawai'i's Own True Sons)*

Motto: Ua Mau ke Ea o ka 'Āina i ka Pono

(The Life of the Land Is Perpetuated in Righteousness)

Demonym: Hawaii resident, Hawaiian

Presidents: Barack Hussein Obama *(44th)*

Quick Fact: *The Hawaiian archipelago comprises 132 islands & islets.*

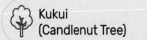 Kukui
(Candlenut Tree)

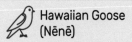 Hawaiian Goose
(Nēnē)

 Hibiscus

IDAHO

GEM STATE

Capital & Largest City: Boise

Date Admitted to Union: July 3, 1890 *(43rd)*

Population: 1,839,106 *(38th Largest)*

Area: 83,569 sq mi (216,443 km2) *(14th Largest)*

State Anthem /Song: "Here We Have Idaho"

Motto: Esto perpetua *(Let it be perpetual)*

Demonym: Idahoan

Quick Fact: Idaho is known as the Gem State, you can find 72 types of precious stones in the state including star garnet (the state gem.) amethysts, rubies, and diamonds.

 Western White Pine   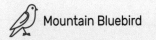 Mountain Bluebird   Syringa

ILLINOIS

ILLINOIS

LAND OF LINCOLN · PRAIRIE STATE
THE INLAND EMPIRE STATE

Capital: Springfield

Largest City: Chicago

Date Admitted to Union: December 3, 1818 *(21st)*

Population: 12,812,508 *(6th Largest)*

Area: 57,915 sq mi (149,997 km²) *(25th Largest)*

State Anthem /Song: "Illinois"

Motto: State Sovereignty, National Union

Demonym: Illinoisan

Presidents: Ronald Wilson Reagan *(40th)*

Quick Fact: The World's Tallest Man, Robert Wadlow was fron Alton. IL. He was 8'11" tall, weighed 491 lbs and wore a size 37 shoe.

 White Oak   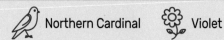 Northern Cardinal   Violet

INDIANA

THE HOOSIER STATE

Capital & **Largest City:** Indianapolis

Date Admitted to Union: December 11, 1816 *(19th)*

Population: 6,785,528 *(17th Largest)*

Area: 36,418 sq mi (94,321 km²) *(38th Largest)*

State Anthem /Song: "On the Banks of the Wabash, Far Away"

Motto: The Crossroads of America

Demonym: Hoosier

Quick Fact: The Indy 500 is an annual automobile race held at Indianapolis Motor Speedway in Indiana. The first race was first held in 1911. Ray Harroun was the first winner. Traditionally since 1936 the race winner drinks a bottle of milk.

 Tulip Tree   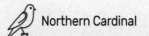 Northern Cardinal   Peony

IOWA

THE HAWKEYE STATE

Capital & Largest City: Des Moines

Date Admitted to Union: December 28, 1846 *(29th)*

Population: 3,190,369 *(31st Largest)*

Area: 55,857.1 sq mi (144,669.2 km²) *(26th Largest)*

State Anthem /Song: "The Song of Iowa"

Motto: Our liberties we prize, and our rights we will maintain

Demonym: Iowan

Presidents: Herbert Clark Hoover *(31st)*

Quick Fact: Iowa is the largest producer of corn in America. 92% of land here is used by farms. The state produces even more corn than some countries including Mexico.

 Bur Oak   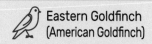 Eastern Goldfinch (American Goldfinch)   Wild Rose

KANSAS

THE SUNFLOWER STATE · THE WHEAT STATE
THE JAYHAWKER STATE

Capital: Topeka

Largest City: Wichita

Date Admitted to Union: January 29, 1861 *(34th)*

Population: 2,940,865 *(35th Largest)*

Area: 82,278sq mi (213,100 km²) *(15th Largest)*

State Anthem /Song: "Home on the Range"

Motto: Ad astra per aspera *(To the stars through difficulties)*

Demonym: Kansan, Jayhawker *(colloquial)*

Quick Fact: Amelia Earhart from Atchison, KS, was the first woman granted a pilot's license & first woman to fly solo over the Atlantic Ocean.

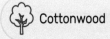 Cottonwood
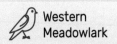 Western Meadowlark
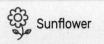 Sunflower

KENTUCKY

BLUEGRASS STATE

Capital: Frankfort

Largest City: Louisville

Date Admitted to Union: June 1, 1792 *(15th)*

Population: 4,509,342 *(26th Largest)*

Area: 40,408 sq mi (104,656 km²) *(37th Largest)*

State Anthem /Song: "My Old Kentucky Home"

Motto: United we stand, divided we fall

Deo gratiam habeamus *(Let us be grateful to God)*

Demonym: Kentuckian

Presidents: Abraham Lincoln *(16th)*

Quick Fact: *By law, Kentuckians must bathe at least once per year.*

 Tulip Tree   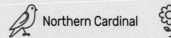 Northern Cardinal   Goldenrod

LOUISIANA

PELICAN STATE · BAYOU STATE · CREOLE STATE
SPORTSMAN'S PARADISE · THE BOOT

Capital: Baton Rouge

Largest City: New Orleans

Date Admitted to Union: April 30, 1812 *(18th)*

Population: 4,657,757 *(25th Largest)*

Area: 52,069.13 sq mi (135,382 km²) *(31st Largest)*

State Anthem /Song: "Give Me Louisiana", "You Are My Sunshine"
"Louisiana My Home Sweet Home", "Gifts of the Earth"

Motto: Union, Justice, Confidence

Demonym: Louisianian, Louisianais *(Cajun/Creole)*, Luisiano *(Spanish)*

Quick Fact: Louisiana is the only state in the union that does not
have counties. Political subdivisions are known as parishes.

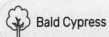 Bald Cypress   Brown Pelican   Magnolia

MAINE

THE PINE TREE STATE
VACATIONLAND

Capital: Augusta

Largest City: Portland

Date Admitted to Union: March 15, 1820 *(32rd)*

Population: 1,362,359 *(42nd Largest)*

Area: 35,385 sq mi (91,646 km²) *(39th Largest)*

State Anthem/Song: "State of Maine"

Motto: Dirigo *("I lead", "I guide", or "I direct")*

Demonym: Mainer, Maine-iac *(colloquial)*

Quick Fact: 90% of the Unites States lobster supply comes from Maine. Approximately 40 million pounds of lobster is caught off the coast.

 White Pine    Chickadee   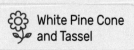 White Pine Cone and Tassel

MARYLAND

OLD LINE STATE · FREE STATE
LITTLE AMERICA · AMERICA IN MINIATURE

Capital: Annapolis

Largest City: Baltimore

Date Admitted to Union: April 28, 1788 *(7th)*

Population: 6,177,224 *(18th Largest)*

Area: 12,407 sq mi (32,133 km²) *(42nd Largest)*

State Anthem /Song: None *("Maryland, My Maryland" until 2021)*

Motto: Fatti maschii, parole femine *(Strong Deeds, Gentle Words)*

Demonym: Marylander

Quick Fact: Annapolis, Maryland, was for a short time the capital of the United States, from 1783–1784.

 White Oak   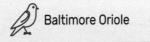 Baltimore Oriole   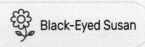 Black-Eyed Susan

MASSACHUSETTS

BAY STATE · PILGRIM STATE · PURITAN STATE
OLD COLONY STATE · BAKED BEAN STATE

Capital & Largest City: Boston

Date Admitted to Union: February 6, 1788 *(6th)*

Population: 7,029,917 *(15th Largest)*

Area: 10,565 sq mi (27,337 km²) *(44th Largest)*

State Anthem /Song: "All Hail to Massachusetts"

Motto: Ense petit placidam sub libertate quietem
        (By the sword we seek peace, but peace only under liberty)

Demonym: Bay Stater, Massachusite *(traditional)*

Presidents: John Adams *(2nd)*, John Quincy Adams *(6th)*, John Fitzgerald Kennedy *(35th)*, George Herbert Walker Bush *(41st)*

Quick Fact: *The first post office in America opened in Boston, MA. in 1639.*

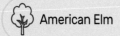 American Elm

 Black-Capped Chickadee

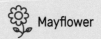 Mayflower

24

MICHIGAN

GREAT LAKE STATE · WOLVERINE STATE
MITTEN STATE · WATER WINTER WONDERLAND

Capital: Lansing

Largest City: Detroit

Date Admitted to Union: January 26, 1837 *(26th)*

Population: 10,077,331 *(10th Largest)*

Area: 99,716 sq mi (250,493 km²) *(11th Largest)*

State Anthem /Song: "My Michigan"

Motto: Si quaeris peninsulam amoenam circumspice

(If you seek a pleasant peninsula, look about you)

Demonym: Michigander, Michiganian, Yooper *(Upper Peninsula)*

Quick Fact: *The name Michigan is from the Native American, 'Mishigami'.*

 White Pine   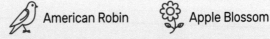 American Robin    Apple Blossom

MINNESOTA

LAND OF 10,000 LAKES
NORTH STAR STATE · GOPHER STATE

Capital: Saint Paul

Largest City: Minneapolis

Date Admitted to Union: May 11, 1858 *(32nd)*

Population: 5,717,184 *(22nd Largest)*

Area: 86,935.83 sq mi (225,163 km^2) *(12th Largest)*

State Anthem /Song: "Hail! Minnesota"

Motto: L'Étoile du Nord *(The Star of the North)*

Demonym: Minnesotan

Quick Fact: Known as the "Twin Cities", nearly 60% of residents live in the Minneapolis – Saint Paul metropolitan area. Minnesota's largest city.

 Norway Pine (Red Pine)

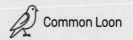 Common Loon

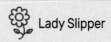 Lady Slipper

MISSISSIPPI

THE MAGNOLIA STATE
THE HOSPITALITY STATE

Capital & Largest City: Jackson

Date Admitted to Union: December 10, 1817 *(20th)*

Population: 2,963,914 *(34th Largest)*

Area: 48,430 sq mi (125,443 km²) *(32nd Largest)*

State Anthem /Song: "Go, Mississippi"

Motto: Virtute et armis (By valor and arms)

Demonym: Mississippian

Quick Fact: Sharkey County, MS. became the birthplace of the Teddy Bear after President Theodore "Teddy" Roosevelt refused to shoot a trapped bear there.

 Magnolia

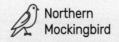 Northern Mockingbird

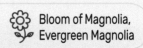 Bloom of Magnolia, Evergreen Magnolia

MISSOURI

SHOW ME STATE · CAVE STATE
MOTHER OF THE WEST

Capital: Jefferson City

Largest City: Kansas City

Date Admitted to Union: August 10, 1821 *(24th)*

Population: 6,160,281 *(19th Largest)*

Area: 69,715 sq mi (180,560 km²) *(21st Largest)*

State Anthem /Song: "Missouri Waltz"

Motto: Salus populi suprema lex esto
   (Let the good of the people be the supreme law)

Demonym: Missourian

Presidents: Harry Truman *(33rd)*

Quick Fact: *Known as the Cave State with more than 6,000 caves.*

 Flowering Dogwood 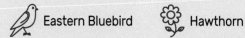 Eastern Bluebird Hawthorn

MONTANA

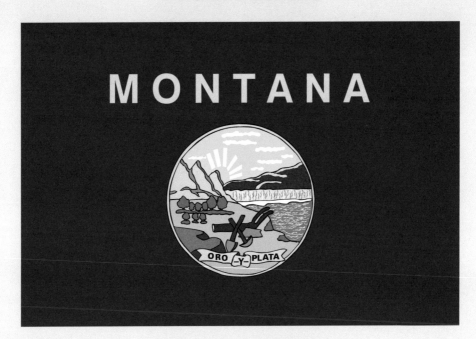

BIG SKY COUNTRY
THE TREASURE STATE

Capital: Helena

Largest City: Billings

Date Admitted to Union: November 8, 1889 *(41st)*

Population: 1,085,407 *(44th Largest)*

Area: 147,040 sq mi (380,800 km^2) *(4th Largest)*

State Anthem /Song: "Montana"

Motto: Oro y Plata" *(Gold and Silver)*

Demonym: Montanan

Quick Fact: Montana's cattle population outnumbers the human population. There are about 2.6 million cattle to the 1.09 million people.

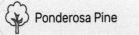 Ponderosa Pine 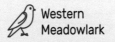 Western Meadowlark  Bitterroot

NEBRASKA

CORNHUSKER STATE

Capital: Lincoln

Largest City: Omaha

Date Admitted to Union: March 1, 1867 *(37th)*

Population: 1,961,504 *(37th Largest)*

Area: 77,358 sq mi (200,356 km²) *(16th Largest)*

State Anthem /Song: "Beautiful Nebraska"

Motto: Equality before the law

Demonym: Nebraskan

Presidents: Gerald Rudolph Ford *(38th)*

Quick Fact: Nebraska has a Navy, but it is triply land-locked. To reach an ocean, you must travel through at least three states.

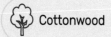 Cottonwood
 Western Meadowlark
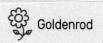 Goldenrod

30

NEVADA

THE SILVER STATE
SAGEBRUSH STATE · BATTLE BORN STATE

Capital: Carson City

Largest City: Las Vegas

Date Admitted to Union: October 31, 1864 *(36th)*

Population: 3,104,614 *(32nd Largest)*

Area: 110,577 sq mi (286,382 km²) *(7th Largest)*

State Anthem /Song: "Home Means Nevada"

Motto: All for Our Country

Demonym: Nevadan

Quick Fact: Las Vegas, NV. is home to over 150,000 hotel rooms - more than anywhere else on Earth.

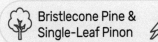 Bristlecone Pine & Single-Leaf Pinon   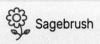 Mountain Bluebird   Sagebrush

NEW HAMPSHIRE

THE GRANITE STATE
THE WHITE MOUNTAIN STATE

Capital: Concord

Largest City: Manchester

Date Admitted to Union: June 21, 1788 *(9th)*

Population: 1,377,529 *(41st Largest)*

Area: 9,349 sq mi (24,214 km^2) *(46th Largest)*

State Anthem /Song: "Old New Hampshire"

Motto: Live Free or Die

Demonym: Granite Stater, New Hampshirite

Presidents: Franklin Pierce *(14th)*

Quick Fact: Named after the county of Hampshire in southern England by Captain John Smith, an English explorer.

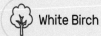 White Birch   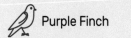 Purple Finch   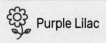 Purple Lilac

NEW JERSEY

THE GARDEN STATE

Capital: Trenton

Largest City: Newark

Date Admitted to Union: December 18, 1787 *(3rd)*

Population: 9,288,994 *(11th Largest)*

Area: 8,722.58 sq mi (22,591.38 km²) *(47th Largest)*

State Anthem /Song: None

Motto: Liberty and prosperity

Demonym: New Jerseyan, New Jerseyite

Presidents: Crover Cleveland *(24nd, 24th)*

Quick Fact: New Jersey is the most densely populated state in the U.S. An average 1,030 people per sq. mi. 13 times the national average.

 Red Oak    Eastern Goldfinch (American Goldfinch)   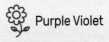 Purple Violet

NEW MEXICO

LAND OF ENCHANTMENT

Capital: Santa Fe

Largest City: Albuquerque

Date Admitted to Union: January 6, 1912 *(47th)*

Population: 2,117,522 *(36th Largest)*

Area: 121,591 sq mi (314,915 km²) *(5th Largest)*

State Anthem /Song: "O Fair New Mexico", "Así Es Nuevo México"

Motto: Crescit eundo *(It grows as it goes)*

Demonym: New Mexican, Neomexicano *(Spanish)*, Neomejicano *(Sp.)*

Quick Fact: Founded in 1610, Santa Fe, NM. is the oldest state capital in the United States, it is also the highest capital city at 2,130 meters (7,000 feet) above sea level.

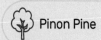 Pinon Pine   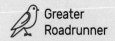 Greater Roadrunner   Yucca

NEW YORK

THE EMPIRE STATE

Capital: Albany

Largest City: New York City

Date Admitted to Union: July 26, 1788 *(11th)*

Population: 20,215,751 *(4th Largest)*

Area: 54,555 sq mi (141,297 km²) *(27th Largest)*

State Anthem /Song: "I Love New York"

Motto: Excelsior *(Ever upward)*

Demonym: New Yorker

Presidents: Martin Van Buren *(8th)*, Millard Fillmore *(13th)*, Theodore Roosevelt *(26th)*, Franklin Delano Roosevelt *(32nd)*, Donald John Trump *(45th)*

Quick Fact: Pinball was illegal in New York City until 1976.

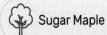 Sugar Maple   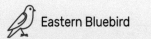 Eastern Bluebird   Rose

NORTH CAROLINA

OLD NORTH STATE
TAR HEEL STATE

Capital: Raleigh

Largest City: Charlotte

Date Admitted to Union: November 21, 1789 *(12th)*

Population: 10,698,973 *(9th Largest)*

Area: 53,819 sq mi (139,390 km²) *(28th Largest)*

State Anthem /Song: "The Old North State"

Motto: Esse quam videri *(To be, rather than to seem)*

Demonym: North Carolinian, Tar Heel *(colloquial)*

Presidents: James Knox Polk *(11th)*, Andrew Johnson *(17th)*

Quick Fact: The Wright Brothers made the first successful powered flight by man at Kill Devil Hill just outside of Kitty Hawk, NC. in 1903.

 Pine   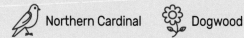 Northern Cardinal Dogwood

NORTH DAKOTA

PEACE GARDEN STATE · ROUGHRIDER STATE
FLICKERTAIL STATE · HEAVEN ON EARTH

Capital: Bismarck

Largest City: Fargo

Date Admitted to Union: November 2, 1889 *(39th)*

Population: 779,261 *(47th Largest)*

Area: 70,705 sq mi (183,123 km²) *(19th Largest)*

State Anthem /Song: "North Dakota Hymn"

Motto: Liberty and Union, Now and Forever, One and Inseparable

Demonym: North Dakotan

Quick Fact: North Dakota became the 39th state on the same day as South Dakota in 1889. Because North Dakota is alphabetically before South Dakota it is listed as 39th state with South Dakota 40th.

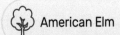 American Elm

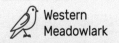 Western Meadowlark

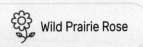 Wild Prairie Rose

OHIO

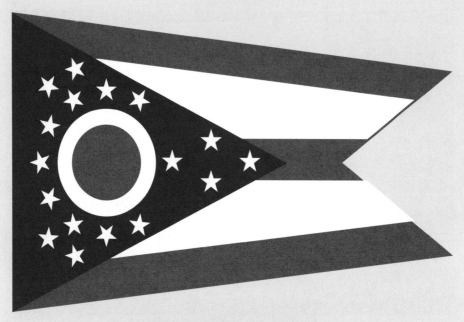

THE BUCKEYE STATE
BIRTHPLACE OF AVIATION · THE HEART OF IT ALL

Capital & Largest City: Columbus

Date Admitted to Union: March 1, 1803 *(17th)*

Population: 11,780,017 *(7th Largest)*

Area: 44,825 sq mi (116,096 km²) *(34th Largest)*

State Anthem /Song: "Beautiful Ohio", "Hang On Sloopy"

Motto: With God, all things are possible

Demonym: Ohioan, Buckeye *(colloquial)*

Presidents: Ulysses S. Grant *(18th)*, Rutherford Birchard Hayes *(19th)*, James Abram Garfield *(20th)*, Benjamin Harrison *(23rd)*, William McKinley *(25th)*, William Howard Taft *(27th)*, Warren Gamaliel Harding *(29th)*

Quick Fact: "Ohio" is from an Iroquois word "Oyo", meaning "Great River".

 Buckeye   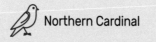 Northern Cardinal    Scarlet Carnation

OKLAHOMA

LAND OF THE RED MAN
THE SOONER STATE

Capital & Largest City: Oklahoma City

Date Admitted to Union: November 16, 1907 *(46th)*

Population: 4,019,800 *(28th Largest)*

Area: 69,898 sq mi (181,038 km²) *(20th Largest)*

State Anthem /Song: "Oklahoma", "Oklahoma Hills"

Motto: Labor omnia vincit *(Work conquers all)*

Demonym: Oklahoman, Sooner, Okie *(colloquial)*

Quick Fact: Oklahoma has more earthquakes than anywhere else in the world, it also has more tornadoes per square mile than any other state of the US.

 Redbud   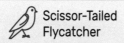 Scissor-Tailed Flycatcher   Mistletoe

OREGON

THE BEAVER STATE

Capital: Salem

Largest City: Portland

Date Admitted to Union: February 14, 1859 *(33rd)*

Population: 4,246,155 *(27th Largest)*

Area: 98,381 sq mi (254,806 km^2) *(9th Largest)*

State Anthem /Song: "Oregon, My Oregon"

Motto: Alis volat propriis *(She flies with her own wings)*

Demonym: Oregonian

Quick Fact: Oregon has a unique state
flag in the U.S., with different designs on
each side. One side shows a state seal
and the other a golden beaver.

 Douglas Fir

 Western Meadowlark

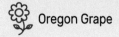 Oregon Grape

PENNSYLVANIA

KEYSTONE STATE
QUAKER STATE

Capital: Harrisburg

Largest City: Philadelphia

Date Admitted to Union: December 12, 1787 *(2nd)*

Population: 13,011,844 *(5th Largest)*

Area: 46,055 sq mi (119,283 km²) *(33rd Largest)*

State Anthem /Song: "Pennsylvania"

Motto: Virtue, Liberty and Independence

Demonym: Pennsylvanian

Presidents: James Buchanan *(15th)*, Joseph Biden Jr. *(46th)*

Quick Fact: The first Zoo in the US opened in Philadelphia, PA. in 1874

 Hemlock   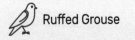 Ruffed Grouse    Mountain Laurel

RHODE ISLAND

THE OCEAN STATE
LITTLE RHODY

Capital & Largest City: Providence

Date Admitted to Union: May 29, 1790 *(13th)*

Population: 1,098,163 *(43rd Largest)*

Area: 1,545 sq mi (4,001 km^2) *(50th Largest)*

State Anthem /Song: "Rhode Island's It for Me"

Motto: Hope

Demonym: Rhode Islander

Quick Fact: Rhode Island is the smallest state in size in the United States. Alaska is the largest. Rhode Island could be fitted into Alaska 425 times.

 Red Maple   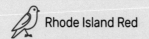 Rhode Island Red   Violet

SOUTH CAROLINA

THE PALMETTO STATE

Capital: Columbia

Largest City: Charleston

Date Admitted to Union: May 23, 1788 *(8th)*

Population: 5,282,634 *(23rd Largest)*

Area: 32,020 sq mi (82,932 km²) *(40th Largest)*

State Anthem /Song: "Carolina", "South Carolina On My Mind"

Motto: Dum spiro spero *(While I breathe, I hope)*

Animis opibusque paratit *(Prepared in mind and resources)*

Demonym: South Carolinian

Presidents: Andrew Jackson *(7th)*

Quick Fact: *South Carolina is the only state with a major tea plantation.*

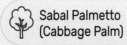 Sabal Palmetto (Cabbage Palm)   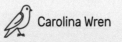 Carolina Wren   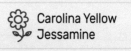 Carolina Yellow Jessamine

SOUTH DAKOTA

THE MOUNT RUSHMORE STATE

Capital: Pierre

Largest City: Sioux Falls

Date Admitted to Union: November 2, 1889 *(40th)*

Population: 909,824 *(46th Largest)*

Area: 77,116 sq mi (199,729 km²) *(17th Largest)*

State Anthem /Song: "Hail, South Dakota!"

Motto: Under God the People Rule

Demonym: South Dakotan

Quick Fact: Most famous for the Mount Rushmore National Memorial, a huge sculpture of George Washington, Thomas Jefferson, Theodore Roosevelt and Abraham Lincoln carved into granite in the Black Hills.

 Black Hills Spruce 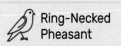 Ring-Necked Pheasant 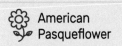 American Pasqueflower

44

TENNESSEE

THE VOLUNTEER STATE

Capital & Largest City: Nashville

Date Admitted to Union: June 1, 1796 *(16th)*

Population: 6,916,897 *(16th Largest)*

Area: 42,143 sq mi (109,247 km²) *(36th Largest)*

State Anthem /Song: "My Homeland, Tennessee", "When It's Iris Time in Tennessee", "My Tennessee", "Tennessee Waltz", "Rocky Top", "Tennessee", "The Pride of Tennessee", "Smoky Mountain Rain", "Tennessee"

Motto: Agriculture and Commerce

Demonym: Tennessean, Big Bender, Volunteer

Quick Fact: Nashville, TN. known as the Music City is considered to be the country music capital of the world, but Bristol, TN. is it's official birthplace.

 Tulip Poplar   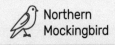 Northern Mockingbird   Iris

TEXAS

THE LONE STAR STATE

Capital: Austin

Largest City: Houston

Date Admitted to Union: December 29, 1845 *(28th)*

Population: 29,145,505 *(2nd Largest)*

Area: 268,596 sq mi (695,662 km²) *(2nd Largest)*

State Anthem /Song: "Texas, Our Texas"

Motto: Friendship

Demonym: Texan, Texian, Tejano *(Spanish)*

Presidents: Dwight David Eisenhower *(34th)*, Lyndon Baines Johnson *(36th)*

Quick Fact: At 268,820 square miles, Texas is larger than many nations of the world, bigger than every country in Europe. If it were a country itself, it would be the 40th largest in the world.

 Pecan   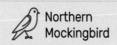 Northern Mockingbird   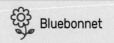 Bluebonnet

UTAH

BEEHIVE STATE
THE MORMON STATE • DESERET

Capital & Largest City: Salt Lake City

Date Admitted to Union: January 4, 1896 *(45th)*

Population: 3,271,616 *(30th Largest)*

Area: 84,899 sq mi (219,887 km²) *(13th Largest)*

State Anthem /Song: "Utah...This Is the Place"

Motto: Industry

Demonym: Utahn, Utahan

Quick Fact: In March 2023 a new flag of Utah was approved, featuring symbols representing various aspects of the state's history, it will be put in use on 9 March 2024.

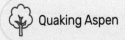 Quaking Aspen   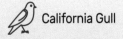 California Gull   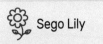 Sego Lily

VERMONT

THE GREEN MOUNTAIN STATE

Capital: Montpelier

Largest City: Burlington

Date Admitted to Union: March 4, 1791 *(14th)*

Population: 643,503 *(49th Largest)*

Area: 9,616 sq mi (24,923 km^2) *(45th Largest)*

State Anthem /Song: "These Green Mountains"

Motto: Freedom and Unity; Stella quarta decima fulgeat

(May the 14th star shine bright)

Demonym: Vermonter

Presidents: Chester Alan Arthur *(21st)*, Calvin Coolidge *(30th)*

Quick Fact: The name Vermont is thought to derive from the French phrase, 'Le Verts Monts". meaning Green Mountain

 Sugar Maple   Hermit Thrush   Red Clover

VIRGINIA

OLD DOMINION · MOTHER OF PRESIDENTS

Capital: Richmond

Largest City: Virginia Beach

Date Admitted to Union: June 25, 1788 *(10th)*

Population: 8,683,619 *(12th Largest)*

Area: 42,774.2 sq mi (110,785.67 km²) *(35th Largest)*

State Anthem /Song: "Our Great Virginia"

Motto: Sic semper tyrannis *(Thus Always to Tyrants)*

Demonym: Virginian

Presidents: George Washington *(1st)*, Thomas Jefferson *(3rd)*, James Madison *(4th)*, James Monroe*(5th)*, William Henry Harrison *(9th)* John Tyler *(10th)*, Zachary Taylor *(12th)*, Woodrow Wilson *(28th)*

Quick Fact: *South Carolina is the only state with a major tea plantation.*

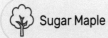 Sugar Maple 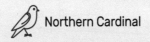 Northern Cardinal American Dogwood

WASHINGTON

THE EVERGREEN STATE

Capital: Olympia

Largest City: Seattle

Date Admitted to Union: November 11, 1889 *(42nd)*

Population: 7,887,965 *(13th Largest)*

Area: 71,362 sq mi (184,827 km²) *(18th Largest)*

State Anthem /Song: "Washington, My Home"

Motto: Al-ki or Alki *(by and by)*

Demonym: Washingtonian

Quick Fact: Washington is the only state that took its name from a President. Shown on the flag and known as the "Father of America," he was president from 1789-1797. The state also has a city named George.

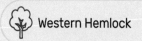 Western Hemlock    Willow Goldfinch (American Goldfinch)   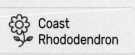 Coast Rhododendron

WEST VIRGINIA

MOUNTAIN STATE

Capital & Largest City: Charleston

Date Admitted to Union: June 20, 1863 *(35th)*

Population: 1,793,716 *(39th Largest)*

Area: 24,230 sq mi (62,755 km^2) *(41st Largest)*

State Anthem /Song: "Take Me Home, Country Roads", "The West Virginia Hills," "West Virginia, My Home Sweet Home", "This Is My West Virginia"

Motto: Montani semper liberi *(Mountaineers Are Always Free)*

Demonym: West Virginian, Mountaineer

Quick Fact: Named after Queen Elizabeth I, known as the 'Virgin Queen'. Nicknamed the Mountain State, West Virginia is the only state completely within the Appalachian Mountain range.

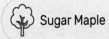 Sugar Maple 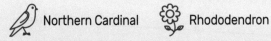 Northern Cardinal 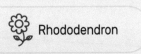 Rhododendron

WISCONSIN

BADGER STATE
AMERICA'S DAIRYLAND

Capital: Madison

Largest City: Milwaukee

Date Admitted to Union: May 29, 1848 *(30th)*

Population: 5,893,718 *(20th Largest)*

Area: 65,498.37 sq mi (169,640.0 km²) *(25th Largest)*

State Anthem /Song: "On, Wisconsin!"

Motto: Forward

Demonym: Wisconsinite

Quick Fact: Wisconsin's nickname comes from the lead miners who traveled here for work in the 1820s. They dug tunnels to find somewhere to sleep and stay warm just like a badger.

 Sugar Maple   American Robin   Wood Violet

WYOMING

EQUALITY STATE
COWBOY STATE · BIG WYOMING

Capital & Largest City: Cheyenne

Date Admitted to Union: July 10, 1890 *(44th)*

Population: 576,851 *(50th Largest)*

Area: 97,914 sq mi (253,600 km²) *(10th Largest)*

State Anthem /Song: "Wyoming"

Motto: Equal Rights

Demonym: Wyomingite, Wyomingian

Quick Fact: Most of Yellowstone, The first National Park in the U.S. It lies within the borders of Wyoming. Approx. 4 million people visit each year. Around 300 species of birds, 67 species of mammals, 16 species of fish, 6 species of reptiles, 5 species of amphibians can be found here.

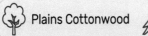 Plains Cottonwood    Western Meadowlark   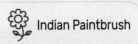 Indian Paintbrush

HISTORICAL STATE FLAGS

Arkansas (1923–1924)

Colorado (1911 - 1964)

Florida (1900 –1985)

Georgia (2001–2003)

Illinois (1915–1969)

Indiana (1903-1917)

Iowa (1917–1921)

Kansas (1927–1961)

Kentucky (1918-1963)

Louisiana (2006–2010)

Maryland (pre-1904)

Massachusetts (1908-1971)

Maine (1901-1909)

Minnesota (1957–1983)

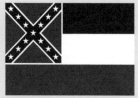

Mississippi (2001-2020)

Montana (1905–1981)

Nebraska (1917–1925)

New Hampshire (1909-1931)

New Jersey (1896–1965)

New Mexico (1912–1925)

New York (1909–2020)

Nevada (1929–1991)

North Carolina (1861–1865)

Oklahoma (1925–1941)

Oregon (1900–1925)

Pennsylvania (1778–1909)

Rhode Island (1882–1897)

South Carolina (1775–1861)

South Dakota (1963–1992)

Tennessee (1897–1905)

Utah (1922–2011)

Vermont (1837–1923)

Washington (1923–1967)

West Virginia (1907–1929)

Wisconsin (1913–1981)

OTHER FLAGS

WASHINGTON D.C. Capital City of the United States

CURRENT UNITED STATES INHABITED TERRITORIES

PUERTO RICO

U.S. VIRGIN ISLANDS

AMERICAN SAMOA

GUAM

NORTHERN MARIANA ISLANDS

STATISTICAL INFORMATION

Admission to Union

1st	Delaware, 1787
2nd	Pennsylvania, 1787
3rd	New Jersey, 1787
4th	Georgia, 1788
5th	Connecticut, 1788
6th	Massachusetts, 1788
7th	Maryland, 1788
8th	South Carolina, 1788
9th	New Hampshire, 1788
10th	Virginia, 1788
11th	New York, 1788
12th	North Carolina, 1789
13th	Rhode Island, 1790
14th	Vermont, 1791
15th	Kentucky, 1792
16th	Tennessee, 1796
17th	Ohio, 1803
18th	Louisiana, 1812
19th	Indiana, 1816
20th	Mississippi, 1817
21st	Illinois, 1818
22nd	Alabama, 1819
23rd	Maine, 1820
24th	Missouri, 1821
25th	Arkansas, 1836
26th	Michigan, 1837
27th	Florida, 1845
28th	Texas, 1845
29th	Iowa ,1846
30th	Wisconsin, 1848
31st	California, 1850
32nd	Minnesota, 1858
33rd	Oregon, 1859
34th	Kansas, 1861
35th	West Virginia, 1863
36th	Nevada, 1864
37th	Nebraska, 1867
38th	Colorado, 1876
39th	North Dakota, 1889
40th	South Dakota, 1889
41st	Montana, 1889
42nd	Washington, 1889
43rd	Idaho, 1890
44th	Wyoming, 1890
45th	Utah, 1896
46th	Oklahoma, 1907
47th	New Mexico, 1912
48th	Arizona, 1912
49th	Alaska, 1959
50th	Hawaii, 1959

Largest by Area

1st	Alaska
2nd	Texas
3rd	California
4th	Montana
5th	New Mexico
6th	Arizona
7th	Nevada
8th	Colorado
9th	Oregon
10th	Wyoming
11th	Michigan
12th	Minnesota
13th	Utah
14th	Idaho
15th	Kansas
16th	Nebraska
17th	South Dakota
18th	Washington
19th	North Dakota
20th	Oklahoma
21st	Missouri
22nd	Florida
23rd	Wisconsin
24th	Georgia
25th	Illinois
26th	Iowa
27th	New York
28th	North Carolina
29th	Arkansas
30th	Alabama
31st	Louisiana
32nd	Mississippi
33rd	Pennsylvania
34th	Ohio
35th	Virginia
36th	Tennessee
37th	Kentucky
38th	Indiana
39th	Maine
40th	South Carolina
41st	West Virginia
42nd	Maryland
43rd	Hawaii
44th	Massachusetts
45th	Vermont
46th	New Hampshire
47th	New Jersey
48th	Connecticut
49th	Delaware
50th	Rhode Island

Largest by Population

1st	California
2nd	Texas
3rd	Florida
4th	New York
5th	Pennsylvania
6th	Illinois
7th	Ohio
8th	Georgia
9th	North Carolina
10th	Michigan
11th	New Jersey
12th	Virginia
13th	Washington
14th	Arizona
15th	Massachusetts
16th	Tennessee
17th	Indiana
18th	Maryland
19th	Missouri
20th	Wisconsin
21st	Colorado
22nd	Minnesota
23rd	South Carolina
24th	Alabama
25th	Louisiana
26th	Kentucky
27th	Oregon
28th	Oklahoma
29th	Connecticut
30th	Utah
31st	Iowa
32nd	Nevada
33rd	Arkansas
34th	Mississippi
35th	Kansas
36th	New Mexico
37th	Nebraska
38th	Idaho
39th	West Virginia
40th	Hawaii
41st	New Hampshire
42nd	Maine
43rd	Rhode Island
44th	Montana
45th	Delaware
46th	South Dakota
47th	North Dakota
48th	Alaska
49th	Vermont
50th	Wyoming

PRESIDENTS OF U.S.A.

	Years	Name	Birth State
1st	1789-1797	Washington, George	Virginia
2nd	1797-1801	Adams, John	Massachusetts
3rd	1801-1809	Jefferson, Thomas	Virginia
4th	1809-1817	Madison, James	Virginia
5th	1817-1825	Monroe, James	Virginia
6th	1825-1829	Adams, John Quincy	Massachusetts
7th	1829-1837	Jackson, Andrew	South Carolina
8th	1837-1841	Van Buren, Martin	New York
9th	1841	Harrison, William Henry	Virginia
10th	1841-1845	Tyler, John	Virginia
11th	1845-1849	Polk, James Knox	North Carolina
12th	1849-1850	Taylor, Zachary	Virginia
13th	1850-1853	Fillmore, Millard	New York
14th	1853-1857	Pierce, Franklin	New Hampshire
15th	1857-1861)	Buchanan, James	Pennsylvania
16th	1861-1865	Lincoln, Abraham	Kentucky
17th	1865-1869	Johnson, Andrew	North Carolina
18th	1869-1877	Grant, Ulysses S.	Ohio
19th	1877-1881	Hayes, Rutherford Birchard	Ohio
20th	1881	Garfield, James Abram	Ohio
21st	1881-1885	Arthur, Chester Alan	Vermont
22nd	1885-1889	Cleveland, Grover	New Jersey
23rd	1889-1893	Harrison, Benjamin	Ohio
24th	1893-1897	Cleveland, Grover	New Jersey
25th	1897-1901	McKinley, William	Ohio
26th	1901-1909	Roosevelt, Theodore	New York
27th	1909-1913	Taft, William Howard	Ohio
28th	1913-1921	Wilson, Woodrow	Virginia
29th	1921-1923	Harding, Warren Gamaliel	Ohio
30th	1923-1929	Coolidge, Calvin	Vermont
31st	1929-1933	Hoover, Herbert Clark	Iowa
32nd	1933-1945	Roosevelt, Franklin Delano	New York
33rd	1945-1953	Truman, Harry	Missouri
34th	1953-1961	Eisenhower, Dwight David	Texas
35th	1961-1963	Kennedy, John Fitzgerald	Massachusetts
36th	1963-1969	Johnson, Lyndon Baines	Texas
37th	1969-1974	Nixon, Richard Milhous	California
38th	1974-1977	Ford, Gerald Rudolph	Nebraska
39th	1977-1981	Carter, James Earl Jr.	Georgia
40th	1981-1989	Reagan, Ronald Wilson	Illinois
41st	1989-1993	Bush, George Herbert Walker	Massachusetts
42nd	1993-2001	Clinton, William Jefferson	Arkansas
43rd	2001-2009	Bush, George Walker	Connecticut
44th	2009-2017	Obama, Barack Hussein	Hawaii
45th	2017-2021	Trump, Donald John	New York
46th	2021-	Biden Jr., Joseph Robinette	Pennsylvania

PRESIDENTIAL FACTS

Republican: Lincoln, Grant, Hayes, Garfield, A. W. Harrison, McKinley, T. Roosevelt, Taft, Harding, Coolidge, Hoover, Eisenhower, Nixon, Ford, Reagan, G.H.W. Bush, G.W. Bush, Trump
Democratic: Jackson, Van Buren, Polk, Pierce, Buchanan, A. Johnson, Cleveland, Wilson, F.D. Roosevelt, Truman, Kennedy, L.B. Johnson, Carter, Clinton, Obama, Biden
Democratic-Republican: Jefferson, Madison, Monroe, J.Q. Adams
Whig: W.H. Harrison, Tyler, Taylor, Fillmore
Federalist: J. Adams
Non-Affiliated: George Washington

Assassinated: Lincoln, Garfield, McKinley, Kennedy
Died 4th of July: Thomas Jefferson, John Adams (1826), John Monroe (1831)
Declaration of Independence drafted by: Thomas Jefferson
Died in Office: W.H. Harrison (1841), Taylor (1850), Lincoln (1865), Garfield (1881), McKinley (1901), Harding (1923), FD. Roosevelt (1945), Kennedy (1963)
Most Terms: FD. Roosevelt (4 terms, died in office 2 months, 23 days of 4th term)
Father/Son Presidents: J. Adams & J.Q. Adams, G.H.W. Bush & G.W. Bush
Nobel Peace Prize Winners: T. Roosevelt, Wilson, Obama, Carter
Oldest to take office: Biden (78 years, 61 days)
Youngest to take office: T. Roosevelt (42 years, 322 days)
Youngest Elected: Kennedy (43 years, 163 days)
Republican Party Symbol: Elephant
Democratic Party Symbol: Donkey

VICE PRESIDENTS

Name	President	Name	President	Name	President
Adams, John	Washington	Wilson, Henry	Grant	Barkley, Alben W.	Truman
Jefferson, Thomas	J. Adams	Wheeler, William A.	Hayes	Nixon, Richard	Eisenhower
Burr, Aaron	Jefferson	Arthur, Chester A.	Garfield	Johnson, Lyndon B.	Kennedy
Clinton, George	Jeff./Madison	Hendricks, Thomas	Cleveland	Humphrey, Hubert	L.B. Johnson
Gerry, Elbridge	Madison	Morton, Levi P.	B.Harrison	Agnew, Spiro	Nixon
Tompkins, Daniel	Monroe	Stevenson, Adlai	Cleveland	Ford, Gerald R.	Nixon
Calhoun, John C.	J.Q. Ads./Jack.	Hobart, Garrett A.	McKinley	Rockefeller, Nelson	Ford
Van Buren, Martin	Jackson	Roosevelt, Theodore	McKinley	Mondale, Walter	Carter
Johnson, Richard	Van Buren	Fairbanks, Charles	T. Roosevelt	Bush, George H.W.	Reagan
Tyler, John	W.H. Harrison	Sherman, James	Taft	Quayle, Dan	G.H.W. Bush
Dallas, George M.	Polk	Marshall, Thomas	Wilson	Gore, Al	Clinton
Fillmore, Millard	Taylor	Coolidge, Calvin	Harding	Cheney, Dick	G.W. Bush
King, William R.	Pierce	Dawes, Charles G.	Coolidge	Biden, Joe	Obama
Breckinridge, John	Buchanan	Curtis, Charles	Hoover	Pence, Mike	Trump
Hamlin, Hannibal	Lincoln	Garner, John N.	F.D Roosevelt	Harris, Kamala	Biden
Johnson, Andrew	Lincoln	Wallace, Henry A.	F.D Roosevelt		
Colfax, Schuyler	Grant	Truman, Harry S	F.D Roosevelt		

MISCELLANEOUS FACTS

Capital of USA: Washington, D.C. (since 1791)
Motto: "In God We Trust"
Currency: U.S. Dollar / Cent
Primary Language: English
UN Member Since: 1945
Type of Government: Federal Presidential Constitutional Republic
National Day: 4 July
National Anthem: "The Star-Spangled Banner"
America named after: Amerigo Vespucci (Italian explorer)
Mayflower Landing: November 21, 1620
GDP: $22.940 trillion
Driving Side: Right
Revolutionary War (War of Independence): 19 Apr 1775 - 03 Sep 1783
Ivy League Universities: Princeton, Harvard, Columbia, Yale, Pennsylvania, University of Dartmouth College, Brown University, Cornell University
Area of North America: 3,796,742 sq mi (9,833,520 km^2)
Population of North America: 331,449,281
Percentage of Earth: 1.927% Earth's total surface area 6.598% of Earth's land area
Borders with Canada: Alaska, Michigan, Maine, Minnesota, Montana, New York, Washington, North Dakota, Ohio, Vermont, New Hampshire, Idaho, Pennsylvania
Borders with Canada: Texas, New Mexico, Arizona, California
Wettest Place: Mt. Waialeale (Hawaii), approx. 460 inches (11.7 mm) rain per year
Driest Place: Death Valley National Park (California) approx 2 inches (50.8 mm) p.y.
Tallest Building: One World Trade Center, New York City 1,776 ft (541 m), since 2014
Longest Tunnel: Delaware Aqueduct (Pennsylvania and New Jersey) 85 miles long and 13.5 feet wide. Longest in the world
Great Lakes: Superior, Michigan, Huron, Erie and Ontario
Islands of Hawaii: Hawai'i, Maui, Kaho'olawe. Lāna'i, Moloka'i, O'ahu, Kaua'i, Ni'ihau
Largest National Park: Wrangell-St. Elias, Alaska, 13004 Sq Mi. (33,682.60 Sq. km)
Highest Mountain: Denali (Mount McKinley), Elevation: 6,190.49 m (20,310 ft) Prominence: 6141 m (20,194 ft), First ascent: 07 Jun 1913
Largest Canyon: Grand Canyon (Arizona), 277 miles (447 km) long, 18 miles (29 km) wide, 6000ft (1.8 km) deep
Longest Mountain Range: Rocky Mountains (Colorado) 3,000 miles (4,800 km)
Longest River: Missouri River, 2,341 miles (3767 km)
Longest Coastline: Alaska, 33904 miles (54,563 km)
NYC Boroughs: The Bronx, Brooklyn, Manhattan, Queens, and Staten Island
Highest Temperature: Death Valley National Park (California) 56.7°C (134°F), 1913
Lowest Temperature: Prospect Creek (Alaska) −80 °F (−62 °C), 1971

Made in United States
Troutdale, OR
10/30/2024

24189438R00038